MW01001874

Love Yourself Again

Love Yourself Again

How to Create Standards, Set Healthy
Boundaries & Stop Being a Doormat

KRYSTLE LAUGHTER

Love Yourself Again: How to Create Standards, Set Healthy Boundaries & Stop Being a Doormat

© 2021 by Krystle Laughter

Published by Krystle Laughter, LLC
Tacoma, WA 98409

Printed in the United States of America

All right reserved. No part of this publication may be reproduced, stored in a retrieval system, or transmitted in any form or by any means-electronic, digital, photocopy, recording, or any other- except for brief quotations in printed reviews, without the prior written permission of the author.

All Scripture quotations, unless otherwise stated, are taken from the New King James Version. Copyright © 1982 by Thomas Nelson, Inc. Used by permission. All rights reserved.

Scripture quotations marked CSB have been taken from the Christian Standard Bible®, Copyright © 2017 by Holman Bible Publishers. Used by permission. Christian Standard Bible, and CSB® are federally registered trademarks of Holman Bible Publishers.

Scripture quotations marked BSB are from The Holy Bible, Berean Study Bible. Copyright ©2016, 2018 by Bible Hub. Used by Permission. All Rights Reserved Worldwide.

Scripture quotations marked (CEV) are from the Contemporary English Version Copyright © 1991, 1992, 1995 by American Bible Society. Used by Permission.

Cover & Interior Design by Krystle Laughter

ISBN 978-1-7346951-5-1

Table of Contents

If you don't learn how to love yourself again, you'll give someone your treasure, and in return, they'll give you their trash

Introduction

I used to live in fear. Fear of not being good enough, fear of not being accepted, fear of not being loved. Fear of being myself. I let people control me with their words, actions, and emotions. I didn't do what was best for me. I did what was best for others. I couldn't remember who I was. My identity was wrapped up in pleasing people.

I thought I had to tolerate toxic behavior to receive love. No matter how much I gave, it was never enough. I finally realized that trying to earn love wouldn't make people love me. It made it easier for them to take advantage of me. When you don't know your worth, you choose relationships that reinforce your feelings of unworthiness.

Real love comes when you stop seeking approval and start loving yourself. Love yourself despite your mistakes. Love yourself despite who hurt you, left you, or abused you. Love yourself even when you don't feel worthy because you've loved those who were unworthy before. If I could go back and tell myself anything, it would be this: Stop trying to be good enough because you'll never be good enough for the wrong people.

You deserve to receive just as much love as you give others. Don't rush love, and never settle.

I Lost Myself

I lost myself
I don't know where I've been hiding
I lost myself
I've been trying hard to find me
I lost myself
In the mess and the stress
I lost myself
I failed my "getting to know me" test
I lost myself
But somehow, I still believe
I lost myself
That it's not too late to recover me
I lost myself
I once was blind, but now I see
I lost myself
It's time for me to be free
I lost myself
I almost gave up hope
I lost myself
I was trying hard just to cope
I lost myself
It's time to be my own best friend
I found myself
Now…I'll never lose myself again

1

Stop Being a Doormat

If you don't learn how to love yourself again, people will mistreat you, and you'll blame yourself

After many years, I finally realized that loving people doesn't mean letting them walk all over you. You don't just have to accept whatever people give you. You have the right to ask for more, get your needs met, and walk away if they're unwilling to treat you right. Before, I was too scared to set boundaries. What if they refused to change? I didn't want to be alone, so I tolerated toxic behavior, hoping my patience would give them time to get their act together and make them love me more. It backfired. The more I gave, the more I was taken for granted. I learned the hard way to love myself because I was all I had.

Losing relationships is painful, but losing yourself is worse. You don't have to tolerate disrespect, manipulation, and narcissism from people who claim to "love" you. People who mistreat you, blame you, and then act like it never happened; that's abuse! The people closest to you should be your biggest supporters, not your greatest offenders. You have to stop participating in toxic behavior. Your presence is participation!

Verbally disagreeing with a toxic person's behavior isn't enough! You have to stand your ground by completely removing yourself from the situation. Be okay with being alone if being alone means you have peace. Loving yourself again means letting go of the toxic people you think you can't live without because you are the only person you really can't live without!

No one benefits when we lose ourselves trying to make them happy, not even the people we think we're doing it for. Every time we shrink to please others, we dishonor ourselves. How you feel is just as important as how they feel. Your needs are just as valid as theirs. When you put their well-being before your own, you reinforce the idea that you aren't worthy of love; that love has to be earned. Stop that! You deserve kindness, empathy, loyalty, and compassion too. You were worthy then, and you're still worthy now. The question is, do you believe it?

When you don't know your worth, you settle for what people give you instead of what you want and need. You desire healthy relationships, but you settle for toxic ones. You want loyal friends, but you tolerate people who gossip about you. You deserve more than what you've been given. It's time to give it to yourself.

Choose People Who Choose You

For you to have better, you have to choose better. You are one hundred percent in control of your adult relationships. You get to choose who you spend your time with. You get to handpick "your" circle. Remember in elementary school when you got to select your team? You only wanted the very best players. You chose your best friends, and the people you knew would help you win.

Adulthood should be the same. Stop picking losing teams. Be honest with yourself about the people you need in your life, and be just as unapologetic about the people you want to keep out. Stop feeling guilty for protecting and prioritizing yourself. If certain people trigger you or turn you off, admit that and honor your feelings. Listening to your intuition will save you time. It will also protect you from dangerous people.

Stop choosing people out of loneliness, fear, and insecurity. The stakes are much higher in adulthood, so you have to be wise. If you want to stop getting hurt, you have to stop choosing the same types of people. Take your time getting to know yourself, learn from your mistakes, and distance yourself from people who aren't good for you. This requires being in touch with yourself.

Let go of one-sided relationships and people who avoid responsibility. Run from these types of people! If they're supposed to be in your life, they will treat you right. No exceptions! Have you ever wondered why the people you're trying so hard to please aren't concerned with pleasing you?

You care about their feelings, but they don't mind hurting yours. You go out of your way for them, but they're never there for you. Something's wrong with this. You deserve better!

Pieces of Me
(Part 1)

Baby Momma Drama, Rejection & Emotional Abuse

Three weeks after we were married, I found out his ex-girlfriend was pregnant, and she thought it was his. It's not what you're thinking. We knew each other for a while, but we were just friends. We began dating in January, and we got married fast, too fast, in March of that same year. She got pregnant in December, right before we started dating. I should have left when I found out but leaving never crossed my mind. I thought that this man was the one.

Looking back, I can see how delusional I was. I didn't even like him at first. It was our female apostle who said that this man was my husband. She announced it in front of the whole church. When she announced it, I was embarrassed and disgusted. I had no interest in this man at all. He was seventeen years older than me, had a receding hairline, and struggled with depression.

At the time, he was staying in a shelter for veterans overcoming drug addiction. He had to lie to stay there. To top it off, he dressed like he was homeless and was socially awkward. No way this could be my husband? Yet, within days of her speaking over me, I began to have feelings for him. Be careful who you let speak into your life.

We began dating and quickly set a date to get married. He didn't propose until a few weeks before the wedding. I should've got a clue when my mom objected and told my brothers and sisters to boycott the wedding. I was upset with them. I didn't understand that they were trying to protect me. On the day of my wedding, none of my family showed up. I didn't care because I was getting my happily ever after, or so I thought.

We took my car on the honeymoon because he let his tabs expire the day before. Less than an hour into the two-hour drive, my car started smoking, and a tow truck had to pick us up. The car was unrepairable. The tow truck driver dropped us off in some small town that shut down daily at seven o'clock. I remember sitting on the side of the road with all of my personal belongings exposed as we waited for a friend to take us on our honeymoon. I was annoyed and angry.

Eventually, we got to our destination, but I was humiliated. It blows me away that I didn't see all of these things as a sign that I'd made a huge mistake. Did I mention that I also planned and paid for the entire wedding, the honeymoon, and the rings? I even picked out my engagement ring; by myself. (I'm shaking my head as I write this. Let my mistakes be your lessons).

After finding out that his ex was pregnant, I was heartbroken. The only person who knew about the situation was our female apostle. She told me that I had to accept the child if it was his because he had accepted my two children. In my heart, I knew this wasn't right because he knew about my children. I felt betrayed and stuck. I didn't know what else to do, so I grudgingly agreed. (This was manipulation. Don't ever let anyone make you feel like you have to accept anything you don't want because you don't. She used her position to intimidate me, and it worked).

The advice I received from her would be the first in a long line of bad advice I got from her and her toxic husband. Unfortunately, at the time, I didn't know any better. I should've left that church, run to the courthouse, and got an annulment, but I didn't. I was determined to make it work. I didn't realize that I was the only one trying.

The child was due in September, and we had to wait until it was born to get a DNA test. I was angry, hurt, and depressed. I was still in school at the time, and the days seemed to drag on. The thought of another woman having my husband's baby was traumatizing. I was jealous. I wanted to be the one pregnant, so I began trying. I realize how stupid this was now, but I was in my feelings at the time. You do dumb things when you're not thinking clearly. Get out of your heart and into your head.

Don't just react to situations. Take some time to think it through, so you can respond wisely.

His pregnant ex-girlfriend called at random to tell him about ultrasounds and how the baby was doing. Whenever she did this, I would object, telling him it was inappropriate and that she should only call when she was ready for him to take the DNA test. He never put her in her place. Eventually, she did stop calling. Those months were some of the most challenging days of my life. All I could do was wait.

September finally rolled around, and the child turned out not to be his. The same month I found out I was pregnant. I was excited. When I shared the news with him, he didn't even pretend to be happy. He didn't say anything at all. I don't know why I didn't get a clue then that this marriage was headed for disaster. I thought all the drama was behind me, but sadly it was only the beginning.

Rejection is a Blessing

Thank God when people reject you because they're doing you a favor. I was blind to my husband's rejection of me. Loving myself would've saved me years of pain. Rejection is more than someone disliking you. It's people withholding love, affection and refusing to meet your needs and respect your boundaries. When people reject you, see their behavior for what it is and let them go. It's better to cry over someone's rejection than to spend the rest of your life crying because you stayed.

Rejection hurts, but disrespect hurts worse. My husband's actions were a sign of his rejection of me. Instead of accepting this, I made excuses for him and deceived myself. I used to think that leaving was the worst thing he could do to me. I found out that rejecting myself to gain his approval was worse; that's self-betrayal. If you have to leave you, to keep them, the price is too high!

If you have to chase someone, they don't want to be caught. Let them go! Please understand that someone's inability to see your value doesn't make you less valuable. There are people who will love you, be loyal to you and meet your needs without making you feel like a burden. You are a blessing! People who reject you are doing you a favor by showing you who they are. Believe them!

Please don't ignore it! Don't try to change them. Keep your dignity and walk away. It will save you from the pain their presence will cause in your life.

Never tolerate someone's rejection because you feel sorry for them either. Brokenness may be their choice, but it doesn't have to be yours. Say this out loud: It's not my job to save anyone! When you make yourself someone's savior, you become their sacrifice. You're not Jesus! You will spend the entire relationship sacrificing your peace, joy, dreams, and happiness, all for someone who will never appreciate it. Refuse to be an enabler. Pick your dignity up off the floor and never look back.

Don't hurt yourself trying to love someone. Love isn't hard! It's only hard when you love someone who doesn't love you in return. Love is easily seen by those who want to receive it. Those who want you to prove your love to them are insecure and seek to control you. That's not love; that's abuse! If someone wants to be in your life, they must treat you right. They need to be patient, kind, considerate, and consistent.

If it's meant to be, it will come with peace. Let me say that again: If it's meant to be, it will come with peace! If it comes with confusion, chaos, heartache, deception, pain, or loss, run! It's not for you! God has something better.

For God is not a God of confusion but of peace.
-1 Corinthians 14:33 (ESV)

What Red Flags Really Mean

We tolerate toxic relationships because we never stop to evaluate what red flags mean. Red flags aren't invitations; they're revelations. We have to stop inviting ourselves into other people's pain. Red flags signify that a person hasn't healed and will hurt us if we continue in the relationship. There were so many red flags in my marriage, but instead of seeing them as warnings, I invited myself in to help. Bad idea! I suffered so much in that relationship. It was a hard lesson, but I know better now.

Imagine driving to a place you've never been to before. As you go, you see signs, but instead of following the directions, you ignore them and try to get there independently. As a result, you are lost, confused, and wondering how you even got there. This is how it is when we ignore signs, aka red flags in relationships.

Red flags give us insight into who a person is beneath the mask. Don't make excuses for them, and never ignore them. Red flags left unchecked and unchanged are dangerous. Their last five relationships failed, and they blamed their exes. They were fired from their previous jobs because their bosses didn't "like" them. Remember, red flags aren't invitations; they're revelations.

Don't hurt yourself trying to love somebody who isn't relationship-ready. Instead, accept the revelation you've been given about them and move on. It's not your job to fix people! It's not your assignment to help someone heal and realize their potential; that's their responsibility. If someone refuses to acknowledge and address their issues, they don't deserve a relationship. It's a sign of their immaturity and a huge red flag.

Adulthood is about accountability and responsibility. If a person is unwilling to accept this for themselves, there's nothing you can do for them. A person who wants a good job will do whatever it takes to get the job they want, whether getting certified or completing a degree program. Similarly, a person who wants to be in your life will do whatever is necessary to keep you in their life.

If there are changes they need to make, they will make them. You won't have to nag or give them ultimatums. If they act like they don't care about losing you, it's because they don't. It's not an act!

Going in Cycles

I know it's hard to hear, but we repeat lessons from which we don't learn. Unfortunately, we won't know what lessons we've failed until we take them all over again. I know it's unfair, but that's just how life works. I didn't realize this until I found myself right back in the middle of another toxic marriage. The lesson I still hadn't learned was self-love. Had I loved myself, I would have never married my ex-husbands.

My second marriage lasted for nine years. I didn't realize that I was being emotionally abused by my husband and the people who counseled us the entire time. They did an excellent job of convincing me that I was overreacting, being unsubmissive, and needed to let him "be the man." He was destroying me mentally, emotionally, and spiritually, but all that seemed to matter was forgiving him and sticking by his side.

By the time I was able to see the situation for what it was, abuse! I had been isolated from my family, had low self-esteem, and lacked self-confidence. I was miserable, angry, and felt hopeless. I'd spent years loving someone who refused to love me in return. I was there for him through his ups and downs, but when I needed him, he was never around.

Looking back, I see how he manipulated me and others around him to get attention whenever he felt like he was losing it. On my first birthday with him, he acted like he was "depressed." As a result, I had to plan my birthday. I took him out to the Olive Garden. I spent the entire time comforting him and trying to cheer him up. I can see how selfish and narcissistic he was now.

At the time, I felt bad for him. That's what toxic people want us to do so that they can play on our emotions. They use your big hearts against us. Please don't fall for it! I thought I could love and pray his issues away.

I thought my love could save him. I learned that you can't save anyone from themselves, and you can't help people who don't want to help.

They have first to help themselves. No amount of praying, sexing, begging, or pleading will be enough to change someone who thinks that there's nothing wrong with them. Don't waste your energy feeling sorry for people who are making you miserable. That's not love! If you see someone trying to sink your ship, why would you keep letting them on board? You will be better off letting them go, as hard as it may be.

Toxic people will use you as long as you allow it. Someone mistreating you requires your participation. You have to remain in their presence for them to do it. Does this mean it's your fault? No! But it does mean that it's your responsibility to protect yourself by removing yourself from the situation when it's safe to do so. I've been in situations where my life was in danger, so I understand entirely feeling stuck. The important thing is that you seek help, make a plan and get out as soon as possible.

Patterns Are Predictors

Pay attention to patterns because patterns are predictors. Patterns reveal how a person will behave based on how they've previously conducted themselves.

How they treat them is how they'll treat you. If they blame them, they'll blame you too. Pay attention to how people speak about people they used to love. What a person says reveals their attitude, character, and values. It tells you who they are and what being in a relationship will be like with them.

It's also vital to assess their current relationships. Do they have friends? Are they close with their family? Who are the primary influences in their life? Are they healthy? How do they view commitment? These questions will help you better picture who you're dealing with. I don't care how attractive a person is, how much money they have, or if you like their personality. If there are red flags, you need to run!

Don't be so in love with the idea of someone that you ignore the reality of who they are. The people you choose will affect every area of your life, for better or worse, so choose wisely.

No More Fixer-Uppers

A fixer-upper is a person who has potential. You see it, but they don't see it for themselves. These types of people constantly make bad choices. They take and take and never give. They make excuses for why their life is the way it is;

it's always someone else's fault. You feel sorry for them, so you keep trying to help them, but you're wasting your time. They're not ready for a relationship.

A person must be able to see their potential and work toward improving themselves. They have to stop making excuses and start making changes. Please don't invest in people who refuse to invest in themselves. Life is hard enough without someone dragging you down with their self-made drama. Dry your tears, cut your losses, and move on!

Don't waste decades of your life waiting, hoping, and pleading for someone to change. That's who they are, and you can't change them. Keep your self-respect and dignity by walking away. People are always showing us who they are. You must pay more attention to a person's actions than words. Words lie, but actions don't!

Chapter 1 Review

Point #1:

There is no benefit to staying in a toxic relationship. Toxic relationships damage our confidence and self-esteem. Allowing people to disrespect you reinforces their bad behavior. You have to stop being a willing participant and remove yourself from the situation. You deserve safe people who love you as much as you love them. Don't settle out of fear.

Point #2:

You're in control of who you allow in your life. To have healthy relationships, you have to choose people who choose you. People who choose you willingly love, respect, and value you. You don't have to chase anyone or prove your worthiness to them. The right people will see it and love you for it.

Point #3:

Rejection is a blessing! When people reject you, they're saving you from hurt and pain, so be thankful for it no matter how much it hurts. Forcing a relationship with a toxic person because you love them is dangerous. You must learn to love yourself the way you want to be loved and let them go.

Point #4:

Red flags aren't invitations; they're revelations. They warn you when something isn't right. Please don't ignore them! You may not get a second chance. Never invite yourself to fix other people's issues. You deserve someone whole, healed & ready! Be okay being alone if being alone means that you're safe and have peace.

2

The 4 Pillars of Self-Love

If you don't learn how to love yourself again, you'll
exchange your power for pain

You are powerful! The power you possess is love. Self-love is your superpower. Loving yourself means respecting your needs, feelings, standards, and boundaries and requiring others to do the same. Although self-love looks different for everyone, its message is identical: I know my worth. I know my value. I know what I bring to the table, and I'm unwilling to settle for less. Take it or leave it.

Self-love is confident, secure, and willing to walk away to protect itself. Self-love is our greatest asset, and its absence will always be felt in our lives. When you lack self-love, you seek validation from others. Working to earn love, which is impossible because love can't be earned; it's given. Take your power back!

Why do we settle? Why do we give so much to people who give us so little in return? The answer is fear. Fear makes us believe that we are unworthy of the things we desire. It makes us think we're asking for too much when we're not asking for enough in most cases. Fear makes us believe that our standards are too high and that no one will meet them. The truth is that toxic people will never rise to the occasion.

Pieces of Me
(Part 2)

Postpartum & Hotel Drama

Four years into marriage and things were not going well. We had just had our third child, our duplex was being renovated, and we were staying in a hotel for two weeks while they finished it. It should've been a peaceful time, but it wasn't. We hadn't even left the complex before the drama began.

He was in one of his unprovoked moods again. It always came out of nowhere. When he got like this, he'd have a nasty attitude, ignore the children and me, and refuse to respond to us when we called him. I didn't know it at the time, but it was emotional abuse. I recognize that he did this anytime he wanted to leave. He'd create a fight and then use it as an excuse to abandon us. On this occasion, he started driving erratically in the parking lot.

He was intentionally swerving and driving recklessly. I told him that if he was going to act like that, I would take the kids to the hotel by myself. I didn't think he'd do it, but he happily stopped the vehicle and fled the car. I was left alone with a two-week-old baby and four young children. I was devastated.

I bawled my eyes out the entire night, trying to figure out how I would care for a newborn, get rest and take care of the other kids. The kids had to be driven to school the following day. The thought of being a single mom was frightening. When he showed up the next day to take the kids to school, I was relieved. I should've planned my exit right then, but I was in no place mentally or emotionally. I was still holding on to hope that my family could be saved.

I hated the way things were, but I felt helpless to change them. I was trying everything I could to make things work, but he was trying everything to make my life a living hell. I was so blind at the time that I couldn't see it. It was like I had been drugged. I dealt with the daily tension by tip-toeing around issues. I knew the way he was behaving was wrong. I didn't know that I had the power to do anything about it. I begged and pleaded with him to act right, to think of our family. He never listened. He always did what he wanted to do. When would I finally do what was best for me?

To be continued …

The Chaos Cycle

Marrying my ex kept me in constant survival mode. I didn't have time to think clearly and rationally. You see, that's what toxic people do. They keep you in what I call "The Chaos Cycle." This cycle comprises four stages: the happy stage, the conflict stage, the convincing stage, and the reconciliation stage.

The Happy Stage

At this stage, things are going well. You have genuinely happy times and are creating good memories. There's no fighting, and you're getting along. It feels like it did initially, and things look like they are getting better. You get excited because it reminds you of how it used to be. You think your pleas have finally been heard, and things will be better now.

The Conflict Stage

In this stage, the toxic person intentionally does something to push your buttons and start arguments. The toxic person's goal is to get you irritated and emotionally agitated. They'll press and provoke you until you react; this eventually happens because you're human and because they've learned exactly what buttons to push. It's also emotional abuse! When you're emotionally distraught, you don't respond; you react.

A response is a well-thought-out, calculated, and intentional action. A reaction is an impulsive decision made with little or no thought of the outcome, and it puts you in a very vulnerable position. Reacting to a toxic person's behavior is a trap!

The Convincing Stage

Once you've responded to their toxic behavior, they will criticize you for how you responded. A toxic person's agenda is to make you feel ashamed and guilty for how you responded to them. The goal is to get the focus off them and on to you. If they can get you to blame yourself for their behavior, they know they can manipulate you. No matter what they do, it will always be your fault. This behavior is both intentional and insidious.

The Reconciliation Stage

In this stage, the toxic person plays the victim by claiming to be deeply affected by your reaction to them, never taking into account their behavior.

They insist that you're the sole cause of the problem and therefore must be the one to change. You feel conflicted because you know you didn't do anything wrong, but their act is so convincing that you still feel guilty. You decide to be the bigger person and apologize to appease them and restore peace to the relationship. By apologizing, you hope to forget what happened and move forward. Your apology only fuels the toxic person because now they know that they can manipulate you. Manipulation equals control.

The cycle starts again because the real issue, their toxic behavior, is never dealt with. Once you recognize that you're in the Chaos Cycle, you need to prioritize your emotional and mental health by getting out of it. This is done through distance. If you can't do this physically, then do it mentally and emotionally. Distancing yourself from a toxic person creates mental and emotional clarity.

A toxic person will never take responsibility for their behavior; they will project it onto you. That's what makes them unhealthy. Trying to reason and rationalize with them will only waste your time and give them another opportunity to manipulate you. Please don't fall for it. You deserve peace. You deserve people who protect you. I know it's hard, but it's what's best for you.

No More Enabling

Taking the blame for things may seem harmless, but it's enabling. You deserve better than that. When you accept responsibility for another person's toxic behavior, you're delaying the ability of that person to change and grow. As long as you allow yourself to be okay with this, you will continue to suffer. Don't accept responsibility for another person's insecurity or actions. You're not crazy or unreasonable for wanting to be treated with the same respect you give to others. You're not selfish for wanting your needs met. You don't have to beg people to treat you right. It is degrading. You don't have to beg for anything; you're not an animal. Anyone who makes you feel like you're not worthy of their time, respect, or attention doesn't deserve you.

People who genuinely care about you will respect you, value you, and honor you. I know it's hard to believe if you've never experienced it, but genuine people are worth waiting for. Don't let toxic people waste your time because you fear being alone. Never fear loneliness. Instead, fear being loyal to people who will never be faithful to you. Fear loving someone who'll never love you in return. Why do we fear being alone so much?

We fear it because we never learned how to love our own company.

We never learned how to be our own friends. Until you know how to love and accept yourself, you'll constantly search for happiness outside of yourself. This is what makes you vulnerable to toxic people. You'll keep finding yourself in unhealthy relationships because you believe that you can't be happy alone. You will hold on to people longer than you should, mistaking enemies for friends and being loyal to people who aren't loyal to you.

Self-love is the foundation of all relationships. When self-love is lacking, all your relationships will be lacking as well. Once you learn self-love, you'll be in the best position to attract healthy relationships because you'll be a healthy person. However, If you don't treat yourself right, you'll eventually accept others not treating you right. Why? Because you've already set the standard. This is why the four pillars of self-love are so important.

The Four Pillars of Self-Love
Pillar 1: Self-Confidence

The first pillar of self-love is self-confidence. Confidence gives you the courage to stand up for yourself and advocate for your needs irrespective of other people's opinions.

Self-confidence helps you set standards and create healthy boundaries. It gives you the courage not to settle and stand your ground when people overstep your boundaries.

Confidence allows you to make reasonable requests of people because you feel worthy of what you're asking for. It helps you trust your intuition, take risks, and let go of people who aren't good for you. People with self-confidence don't blame themselves when people reject them; that's self-defeating. Instead, they focus on how they feel about themselves and their worthiness to be treated right.

Everyone feels insecure at times. The difference is that confident people don't let their feelings control them. Feelings change from moment to moment and day to day, but confidence is a choice. Decide to believe in yourself and to work on your weaknesses. Be confident despite how you feel.

Self-Confidence Affirmations

- I have confidence in my ability to decide what's best for me, at all times and in every situation.
- No one can look out for me better than me
- I am worthy of love. I am deserving of love
- I don't chase love; it chases me

Pillar #2: Self-Development

The second pillar of self-love is self-development. Self-Development is anything you do to improve yourself. It can look like joining a gym, adopting healthier eating habits, learning a new skill, or removing toxic people from your life. It's also going to therapy, unlearning bad habits, and prioritizing your mental health. Self-development is a lifelong commitment.

Self-development is about learning how to love and accept yourself as you are. It should never become an obsession. There will always be something you feel you need to improve. Self-confidence is there to help you evaluate where you are and where you want to be. Reading this book is a form of self-development. You're learning how to heal, love yourself and establish healthy relationships.

Self-development isn't always easy; sometimes, it's uncomfortable. It requires you to leave your comfort zone. It requires you to challenge yourself. Whatever you need to work on, know that you are worth the time and effort to accomplish what you desire. Self-development is self-love.

Self-Development Affirmations

- I am worth the time and effort it takes to love me
- I prioritize myself and my health because I am important
- I'm not where I want to be, but I'm on my way there
- I love investing in myself
- I am amazing

Pillar #3: Self-Respect

The third pillar of self-love is self-respect. Respect is the politeness, honor, and care you show towards something or someone you consider important. When you respect someone, you're careful with that person, but not in a fearful way. We don't want to do anything to hurt that person because we care about their feelings. We think highly of them and go out of our way to honor them.

As you learn to respect yourself, consider how you demonstrate respect to others. How do you speak to them? What tone of voice do you use? How do you respond when they make a mistake? Whatever you'd do for them, do the same for yourself.

At first, it may be challenging to respect yourself; that's okay. Just as people-pleasing develops over time, learning how to respect yourself will take time.

Start small and be consistent. The slow and steady change will help you build the momentum to sustain it.

Self-respect is evident in how we carry ourselves and how we treat others. People who respect themselves have no problem respecting others. To be successful, you must define what self-respect means to you.

Self-Respect Affirmations

- I am respectful
- I am respectable
- I respect myself
- It's easy for others to respect me
- I am worthy of respect
- I am proud of myself
- I honor me

Pillar #4: Self-Preservation

Self-preservation is the intentional act of protecting yourself from harm. It's stopping at a red light. It's putting your seatbelt on. It's listening to your intuition when something doesn't feel right. It's calling the police when you feel threatened. A healthy and natural response to a threat is self-preservation.

Although self-preservation is instinctual, it can be hindered through abuse and exposure to toxic people. Toxic people train you to question yourself. They make you doubt your sense of reality and your version of events (Known as gaslighting). Toxic people manipulate you by blaming, shaming, accusing, and criticizing you. They withhold affection, affirmation, and attention, refusing to meet your needs until you comply with their demands.

Practicing self-preservation will help you break free from toxic and abusive cycles. Instead of trying to preserve relationships with toxic people, make it a priority to protect your peace, dignity, and sanity. Don't let pleasing them be your concern any longer. They had their chance. Make yourself the top priority. Shift your focus from we-centered to "me-centered."

Before agreeing to any request, ask yourself this: will this harm my mental or emotional health? If so, refuse to do it. You don't have to apologize, no need to feel guilty. You have a right to do what's best for you the way you've done what's best for others. The people who care about you will understand and encourage it.

Self-Preservation Affirmations

- It's an honor to protect myself
- I always do what's best for me

- I'm not afraid to make decisions that protect my mental and emotional health
- I choose safe and healthy relationships
- I value people who make me feel safe
- I trust myself
- I am my own best friend
- I won't hesitate to protect myself from disrespectful, dishonest, and dangerous people

Relationships Are Reflections

Your relationships are reflections of the relationship you have with yourself. When you respect yourself, you require others to respect you too. Self-love prevents you from tolerating people who abuse, belittle and mistreat you. When you lack self-love, you feel insecure and unworthy. You seek out relationships to make you happy. Leaving you vulnerable to toxic people. You may allow people to mistreat you because you feel like you "need" them. News Flash: You don't need them, and you never did. Take back your power! Don't let fear and unworthiness keep you stuck.

You are a valuable addition to the lives of the people around you. You have to stop seeing everyone else as the prize. You are a prize too!

Similarly, people in close relationships should possess similar characteristics and values that align with who they are and what matters most to them. If you value loyalty and honesty, then the people around you should value loyalty and honesty. If you're a supportive person, surround yourself with supportive people too.

Understand that not everyone will value you. That's a good thing because it indicates who does and doesn't belong in your life. When people don't respect your boundaries, pay attention. Their actions reveal their character. A person's character is important because it's who they are.

Without Walls

A city without walls is quickly overtaken, and a house with a door is not hard to rob. Imagine going into a jewelry store with no security system. The beautiful glass-lit cases sparkle with diamonds, gold, and colorful gems. As you admire the jewelry, you overhear the store owner saying that he doesn't have any locks for the jewelry cases. He also can't afford a security guard or a lock for the door either.

Unbeknownst to the jeweler, a thief is in the jewelry store and overhears the conversation. The next day when you return to the store to buy jewelry, you find broken glass, yellow tape, and police cars surrounding the building; the store has been burglarized.

The owner failed to protect his precious treasures. Like the jewelry store owner, we fail to defend ourselves when we lack self-love. It's not that toxic people are drawn to you; you don't have anything to keep them out.

Self-love protects you from toxic people. The goal of toxic people is to use and manipulate others. Self-love filters toxic people out of your life. They'll either leave your life or change when they see that they can't mistreat or take advantage of you. Either way, you win.

Chapter 2 Review

Point 1:

Self-love is the answer you've been looking for. The Four Pillars of Self-Love will help you put self-love into action. Self-confidence will give you the courage to ask for what you want and the faith to wait for it. Self-development will help you build discipline and endurance to establish healthy habits that improve your life for the better. Self-respect will teach you to value yourself, preserve your dignity while increasing your self-esteem.

Self-preservation will protect you by alerting you of potentially dangerous situations, circumstances, and people. Trust your intuition and listen!

Point 2:

The Chaos Cycle keeps you in a never-ending loop of emotional distress. When you recognize yourself in this cycle, break free from it by removing yourself from the relationship. Don't waste your time trying to reason and rationalize with a toxic person. It doesn't work; it gives the toxic person a chance to bait you back in, using guilt and pity.

Point 3:

Your relationships are a reflection of the relationship you have with yourself. When we lack self-love, we choose people who lack love for us. When we don't have a strong foundation of self-love, we don't know what someone else loving us looks like. Let your relationships reflect the love, honor, and respect that you have for yourself. Let go of people who shame and manipulate you. Choose people who treat you the way you deserve to be treated.

Point 4:

No more enabling! We enable people when we take responsibility for their actions, abuse, and shortcomings. You're not to blame for another person's actions. You're not wrong for responding to someone's insults and disrespect. Stop blaming yourself and stop letting people shame you for protecting yourself.

3

You Get What You Settle For: Creating Standards

If you don't learn how to love yourself again, you'll settle for suffering instead of creating standards

In life, you don't get what you deserve. You don't even get what you demand. In life, you get what you settle for. When you don't know your worth, you live in a constant state of anxiety. You fear not being good enough. You question your value. You wonder if anyone will truly love you. In an attempt to win people's affection, you'll ignore red flags, overlook disrespect, and forget the standards you once held. Don't do this! You are valuable. You don't have to wait for someone to love you. You can love yourself. Refuse to settle for less than you deserve.

What have you settled for? Toxic relationships, bad habits, or low self-esteem? We often look at other people's success as if they've always been that way. We don't realize that every person has overcome obstacles to get to where they are. If you want high-quality relationships, you have to overcome your fear and create high standards.

If you want relationships with healthy people, you have to choose healthy people. You have to be intentional. If you want relationships with kind and considerate people, you have to choose kind and thoughtful people. This is why taking your time to get to know people is essential. Anyone can pretend to be what you want for a season. Be patient and keep your guard up until they prove themselves.

Frequently, we get involved with people, only to find out later they're not who we thought they were. We then try to change them to make us happy, but they resist. People are already who they are. You have to accept this and resist the urge to change them. It's painful to realize someone you love is toxic, but holding on to them will only hurt you. Love yourself enough to let them go.

Never Settle

When you release people and create standards, you're practicing self-love. Love is an action word. When you create standards, you're setting the bar for all of your relationships.

When someone doesn't meet your standards, don't settle. Don't make excuses for them either. You'll only end up regretting it later. Communicate your standards and see if they will rise to your level. Never sink to theirs.

For instance, someone likes you, but they smoke. Your standard is someone who values their health; a non-smoker. Explain to the person that you don't date smokers because you value your health, and you want someone who values it too. Don't expect people to change for you. If they do, great. If not, you've lost absolutely nothing. You now know that they're not right for you. Move on!

When you're tempted to settle for less, stop to imagine how your life would be if you settled. Pause and consider:

1. What will I be giving up to be with this person? My standards and values? My health and self-respect?
2. What will I have to tolerate in a relationship with this person? Criticism, lack of trust, etc.?
3. What will my life be like with this person? Happy or sad? Fulfilled or unsatisfying?
4. How will I feel in 10 years? Shame and regret or joy and peace?
5. How will it affect me and/or my children? Is it worth it?

When you take the time to count the cost of settling, you'll realize that the price is too high. You are worth the standards you set. If you settle, you'll never know what you could've had if you waited. Don't live a life of regret. When you lack standards, you let people have access to you that shouldn't. You have few requirements because you're desperate for anyone's company. Treating relationships so casually will cost you. Practice the Four Pillars of Self-Love. Prioritize yourself and the things that matter to you. You deserve to get what you want too.

Be wise and intentional about who you choose. The people in your life should reflect your standards, morals, beliefs, and values. This is not to say that you can't have differences, but you should hold the same core values if you want to enjoy a peaceful relationship. If family is important to you, it should be important to the one you're with. If faithfulness is non-negotiable, don't tolerate someone who cheats on you.

If you can't accept someone's behavior, mindset or attitude, it will cause constant conflict. Choose peace and leave the relationship before you waste any more time. A part of life is losing relationships and embracing new ones. Mourn your losses, then celebrate new opportunities. You'll find the people who are right for you, but first, you must let go of the wrong ones.

Pieces of Me
(Part 3)

Porn, Lust & No Sex

In the beginning, it seemed like we had so much in common. We liked the same movies, had the same views, and went to the same church. He came across as extremely funny, helpful, and attentive. After marriage, I quickly realized that he was not who he pretended to be. His bubbly, outgoing life of the party personality was just an act.

At home, he had little to nothing to say. He was solemn, cold, and distant. As soon as we got around strangers, he was back to performing. He'd crack jokes, make people laugh, and be over the top. It was embarrassing and made me uncomfortable. Everywhere we went, he tried to get attention. I thought it was weird, but I brushed it off (Never ignore your intuition).

We couldn't just go out and have an evening to ourselves. He had to be loud and attract attention from everyone around him (People who need constant attention are insecure people). IT WAS AN ENTIRELY DIFFERENT STORY when I tried to be playful behind closed doors. I was met with disdain and disinterest. I was hurt and confused.

Additionally, I was the one who initiated intimacy. I would dress up, put on romantic music, and light candles. He frequently rejected me, saying he was too tired and wanted to talk. I later realized it was because he was watching pornography. We would go months without sex because of this. I decided to seek outside help.

We ended up being counseled by the female apostle of our church and her husband. They had known my husband for a decade, and she married us. When she married us, she was divorced from her husband who had asked her for a divorce. The couple I wanted to counsel with had been married for over twenty years; we're happily married and had advised us both privately before.

I was met with opposition by my husband and both of the apostles. They told me I could only receive counseling from them because the wife was the one who married us. Something didn't seem right. My husband also didn't want me talking to the other couple's husband, even though he frequently spoke to the female apostle alone. I knew this was unfair and hypocritical, but I obliged because I wanted to honor my husband (Honor those who honor you).

The other married couple warned me that it wasn't wise to do what my husband was asking me, but I didn't listen. It turned out to be the worst decision of my life. With the married couple I trusted out of the way, I had no one looking out for me. My husband's cold and distant attitude grew worse. The apostles who counseled us were extremely inconsistent and always sided with my husband.

My husband continued to create conflict with his passive-aggressive attitude and porn addiction. Whenever I tried to talk to him about improving our relationships, family, or finances, he would literally fall asleep.

He was always too busy to spend time with us when he was awake, although he seldomly held a job. I walked on eggshells to keep the peace. To top it off, his issue with lust was becoming unbearable. It got to the point where I stopped wanting to go anywhere because he was always looking at other women.

Looking back, I realized that I was suffering from anxiety and depression. I stopped planning vacations, dates, and outings. I stopped planning family vacations. I stopped dreaming. I avoided crowded places and beaches, anywhere there might be opportunities for him to have wandering eyes. I was desperately trying to preserve my marriage. I should have been practicing self-respect and self-preservation by leaving.

Despite all of the hardships, we still had happy moments. I say moments because it never lasted long. Those times gave me hope and kept me hanging on (The Chaos Cycle). I knew it would get better, even if for a week or two. That's usually how short the peace lasted. He would isolate himself for hours in the laundry room with the excuse that he was washing clothes. That's where he'd watch pornography.

During the happy times is when I would get pregnant. That was one thing he did well, knock me up. I wish I had loved myself enough to stop giving him access to me sexually, but it was the only time I felt connected to him.

After discovering I was pregnant, he'd distance himself again and go into a pity party, making everything about him. It was disgusting.

When I was pregnant, I went to most appointments alone. I felt unwanted and rejected. It was crazy. I don't know how I stayed for so long. I think I held on because I believed that God could change him. I failed to realize that God doesn't change people who don't think they need help. He was steadily getting worse, and I was tired. He would blow up and leave for days without letting me know where he was.

I was desperate to keep my family together. I didn't want to go through another divorce. I didn't want my kids growing up in a broken home, and I didn't want to be a single mom. I failed to realize that I was already living a single life. I took care of the kids, did the budgeting, planning, preparing, and most of the cooking.

I made sure everyone had everything they needed. It was exhausting. I also took care of birthdays and holidays. It was rare when he got me a Christmas gift or a birthday present. I spent most birthdays alone, trying to make the best out of a bad situation.

He never put me first. How long could I endure this madness? When would I finally choose myself?

Standards

I had no standards when it came to my relationship with my ex-husband. Whatever he did, I tolerated it. I cried, complained, and pleaded, but I never left. I never said enough is enough. Similarly, I had no standards for the people who counseled us. I had reservations about the whole situation, but I ignored my intuition and proceeded.

The prudent person sees trouble ahead and hides, but the naive continue on and suffer the consequences.
-Proverbs 22:3 (ISV)-

If I would've taken the time to properly assess the situation instead of trying to please my husband. I would've seen that I was putting myself in a vulnerable situation. The recently remarried apostles had no business counseling us. They didn't have a good track record, their marriage wasn't healthy, and they were displaying controlling and manipulative behavior, which is spiritual abuse.

Self-love protects you. Standards safeguard you. People who lack these things suffer unnecessary harm. It's not your fault that you were never taught these things; I wasn't either. Now that you do know, you have an obligation to protect yourself, put yourself first, and love yourself.

What have you experienced that you could've avoided by simply loving yourself? Let self-love protect you. Let your standards shield you from unnecessary pain.

Creating Your Standards

Setting and maintaining your standards is the key to self-love and healthy relationships. Standards are requirements someone must possess to have a relationship with you. Sometimes we don't know what we want until we've experienced what we don't want. Don't let that discourage you! Once you realize you never want to experience something again, create a standard for that.

Below is an example of standards. You can add these to your list or make your own. Remember, standards should focus on character and values. Who you want them to be, and not what you want them to have. Possessions can be acquired, but character is something that's built over time. It's the difference between a Michael Kors and a Gucci bag; the quality is incomparable.

When thinking about the quality of relationships you want, assess what character traits a person needs to possess to attain it. Those traits should become your standards. Below are a few of my standards. Remember, your standards are specific to you. They won't look like anyone else's. They should be your non-negotiables.

Dating Standards
(Examples)

Financial Responsible

Independent

Healthy Communicator

Mentally Stable

Physical Attraction

Kind

Patient

Respectful

Confident

Loyal

Faithful

Flexible

Consistent

Empathetic

Gentle

Basic Relationship Standards
(Examples)

Positivity

Trustworthy

Honesty

Non-Competing

Non-Judgmental

Compassionate

Supportive

Loyalty

Empathetic

Encouraging

Now that you've seen an example of standards, it's time for you to create your own. Write them down below, put a copy on your phone. Please post them in your office or home where you can look at them. Remember, standards are attributes someone must already possess. They are the requirements you set for people interested in having a relationship with you.

My Dating Standards:

_____

_____

_____

_____

_____

My Relationship Standards:

_____

_____

_____

_____

_____

Remember, you don't get what you deserve. You get what you settle for.

Identify Your Preferences

Most people confuse preferences with standards. What's the difference between standards and preferences? Standards are nonnegotiables, and preferences are optional. A tall, dark, and handsome, six-figure earning man is a preference. A financially stable, goal-oriented man you're physically attracted to is a standard.

The difference between preferences and standards is that one is based on wants, and the other is based on needs. You need to be attracted to your partner. You don't need him to look like your favorite movie star. You need him to be emotionally available. You don't need him to like the same music as you.

Although physical attraction is essential, a person's character is what counts. Looks will eventually fade. What remains is what will dictate the longevity and happiness of your relationship.

Exchanging Treasure for Trash

Imagine giving someone diamonds and them giving you a bag of trash in return. When you give someone something good, you expect appreciation and gratitude. When we give good things to toxic people, they don't value it, and they take it for granted.

They figure out more ways for us to give them what they want while simultaneously giving us less and less. If a person isn't willing to make adjustments to better the relationship, it has to end.

Changing bad attitudes and behaviors is non-negotiable if someone cares about a relationship. Unfortunately, in toxic relationships, the healthy person usually makes the changes. Compromising your standards to sustain unfulfilling relationships is never a good idea. Stop that!

Toxic relationships are one-sided. The people you're doing all the changing for aren't willing to change for you. It's unfair, childish, and unacceptable. I don't care if you're married, dating, or engaged. If they don't give you the same respect they're asking for, don't waste your time with them; they don't deserve you.

Giving people more of what they don't value won't make them appreciate it more. As long as you're willing to accept less than you deserve, there will always be someone ready to give it to you. Stop making it easy for people to take advantage of you. You deserve so much more!

Be Audacious

audacious: showing a willingness to take surprisingly bold risks.

Standards are the foundation of your relationships. You're building on a solid foundation when you set them and require people to meet those standards. You're sending the message that: I am valuable. I am worthy. I am enough. You can't lose when you love yourself like this. People who think you're doing too much are the ones missing out. You keep loving yourself, sticking to your standards, and remembering your value.

While you're waiting for the right people to present themselves, work on yourself. Let the world see that you are in love with yourself!

Chapter 3 Review

Point 1:

You don't get what you want or demand; you get what you settle for. Stop expecting people to be what you need when you don't require anything from them. If you want people that possess certain qualities, you have to choose people who have those qualities. Take your time and don't rush because people will eventually reveal who they are.

Point 2:

When you lack standards, you accept bad treatment because you fear being alone. You must overcome your fear of people rejecting you and not meeting your standards. People who don't honor your standards aren't right for you anyway, so don't be angry. Be thankful that you learned it sooner rather than later, and move on!

Point 3:

Creating standards is essential to love yourself and to have healthy relationships. Sometimes you won't know that you need to set a standard until you've had a bad experience.

Don't be discouraged by this. Create your standards and learn from your mistakes.

Point 4:

Identify and distinguish preferences from standards. A preference is something you want. A standard is something you need. Standards are more important than preferences because they deal with who a person is on the inside; their character. Preferences are more superficial and deal with outward characteristics like physical appearance.

4

Let Them Be Offended: Setting Healthy Boundaries

If you don't learn how to love yourself again, you'll exchange boundaries for breakdowns

Boundaries are guidelines, rules, or limits created to identify safe and reasonable ways for others to treat you. They help others identify what behaviors are acceptable and unacceptable. They let others know how you want to be treated by them. Boundaries protect you from being used, manipulated, and violated by others.

People who have problems with your boundaries usually lack their own. They may disagree with you blatantly or by ignoring them. Either way, you must address it. Once you've made a particular boundary clear, it's up to that person to respect it.

If they choose not to respect your boundaries, they're showing you who they are and that they don't deserve to be in your life.

Never be afraid to communicate your boundaries to others. People can't honor boundaries that they don't know to exist. Sharing your boundaries should happen naturally as situations arise. Without mutual respect, a relationship is doomed to fail or be miserable at best. It doesn't matter if it's friendship, business, or romantic; without boundaries, a relationship will fail.

Everyone wants to be heard. Everyone wants to feel valued by the people they care about. When someone ignores your boundaries, they consciously choose not to value you, making the relationship unsafe. You deserve to feel safe in your relationships. You deserve honor. The people who want a relationship with you should respect your boundaries; it's non-negotiable

How to Communicate Using R.O. A. R

Communication is the lifeblood of relationships. Without it, a relationship dies. It's our job to communicate our needs to the people in our lives. It's their job to listen and to respond appropriately. Communication makes people aware of our needs. Requesting makes us sure we've been heard.

Observation lets us know how others have perceived our needs. Assessment helps us decide how we want to proceed. Responding is the action we take based upon the information we've gathered and our perception of a person or situation.

Request. Communicate your specific need to the person. Explain what you need and why. Don't assume the person already knows, and avoid blaming or criticizing.

Observe. Observe the person's response. What does their body language say? Do they seem open or defensive? Are their responses positive or negative?

Assess. Based on how the person responds to your request, assess whether the person is receptive to you and your needs. If someone gets angry, defensive, or critical of your request, they most likely won't be willing to honor that request.

Respond. Your response will be based on your observation and assessment of the encounter. Their response determines if you should continue, distance, or release yourself from the relationship. If someone resists acknowledging your feelings and needs, then that person is emotionally unsafe. The behavior must change for the relationship to continue.

Pieces of Me
(Part 4)

Abandonment, Death, and a Broken Foot

He was gone! I didn't know where he was for four days. He decided to stay at a homeless shelter than be with his family. Our youngest was six months old, and we had five other children. He left because I asked him to find out what happened first instead of accusing the kids of doing things. I was very relaxed and calm when I spoke to him. (I know that I was being very reasonable, rational, and respectful because toxic people teach you to be overly self-conscious and self-critical).

Instead of listening, he used it as an opportunity to be vindictive and leave. He ignored my phone calls for four days straight. When he finally answered his phone, I asked him why he didn't return. He said it was because I told him not to come back until he calmed down. Another way to project his behavior onto me. Ugh! I was so tired of this game. No matter what he did, he always found a way to avoid responsibility and blame someone else.

To top it off, his mother was seriously ill in the hospital when he left. She was on life support, and the doctors said she didn't have much time to live. They told him that he should make arrangements to see her as soon as possible. I agreed. He said that Apostle Kevin said he shouldn't go to see her because when his mother was sick in the hospital, she died before he could get there. I thought this was stupid. I told him he should see his mother. She was asking specifically for him.

He didn't have the best relationship with her, but it was the right thing to do. He refused. I didn't say anything else after that. I didn't understand how anyone could treat their mother that way.

I couldn't understand how he could abandon us when we needed him most. This was not the first time, so I don't know why I was surprised. The doctors were calling to get a hold of him, but I didn't know where he was or when he'd be back. I eventually had to tell them that my husband was mentally and emotionally unstable and in no condition to make decisions for his mom.

His father, who was still legally married to his mother, stepped in to make decisions for her. They had been estranged for over forty years. I knew that she wouldn't have wanted that, but I was helpless to do anything about it. When I spoke to his father, I asked that I be able to say goodbye before she passed away. He agreed. Weeks later, I found out that she died, no phone call, no goodbye. I was numb at this point. I didn't even have time to process anything because I was still trying to get him to come home. I was angry and confused.

Then it happened. One night while I was putting the kids to bed, I slipped and fell on a toy and violently crashed into the doorway. I couldn't move. The kids had to call the ambulance. I lay there crying, not because of the pain, but because I had no one to care for me.

I didn't know how I would take care of my children with a broken foot. I felt helpless and alone. What was I to do?

... *To be continued.*

The Purpose of Boundaries

...He set a boundary for the sea so that the water would not violate His command when He marked out the foundations of the earth...
-Proverbs 8:29 (NASB)

Boundaries are necessary because they protect you from people with hidden motives and bad intentions. People who want to use and abuse you aren't just going to come out and say that. They will pretend to be everything you want, the answer to your prayers: your knight in shining armor. They will take the time to learn what you like, what you want, and what you need. Once you begin to develop feelings for them, they will use their knowledge against you, playing on your deepest insecurities and fears.

Boundaries help you differentiate between safe and unsafe people. Safe people respect your individuality, your feelings, opinions, and experiences. Dangerous people have a problem with your independence because it threatens their ability to manipulate and control you. They'll push and push your boundaries until you have no left. Don't let anyone do this to you. Take your power back and get out! It's not too late! You can be happy, safe, and free of toxic people.

Your boundaries will offend some people, but that's a good thing. When your boundaries offend others, they're doing their job. They're alerting you of toxic people. It's okay for people to be offended. A person's response to your boundaries has nothing to do with you. It has everything to do with their lack of growth and maturity.

You're not responsible for people's unwillingness to accept your boundaries. Trying to force someone to respect you is a waste of time; they either will or won't. You're only responsible for yourself. Period! If someone takes issue with your boundaries, they're the one with the problem, and that's okay. If someone decides to leave you because of your boundaries, you've successfully rid yourself of a toxic person. Good for you!

Boundaries protect you from people who deny your right to be respected and your need to feel valued. People who are used to abusing and mistreating you will be angry when you won't accept their toxic behaviors anymore. They may yell, curse, lie and even make stuff up to convince you that you're terrible. Please don't fall for it!

Stop expecting mature and rational behavior from toxic people. Stop expecting them to understand your point of view. Stop expecting them to empathize and sympathize with you. A toxic person's focus will always be self-centered.

Stop expecting them to act with your best interest in mind. I know it's hard to hear because you want them to love and support you the way you've loved and supported them, but they are incapable or unwilling to do that.

We only hurt ourselves when we try to force people to be something they aren't. People have free will. They can change or remain exactly as they are. Change is hard. Change is painful. This is why most people stay the same. I am proud of you for choosing change. Be proud of yourself too.

You can no longer allow people who aren't concerned about your mental, emotional and physical health to take up space in your heart and life. They don't deserve you! You deserve people who are genuinely concerned about your well-being. Evaluate your relationships, and do what is necessary to keep your peace and to heal from toxic people. Don't fear being alone when you cut toxic people out of your life. Know that you're making room for the right people. People who will treat you right.

Setting Healthy Boundaries

How do people accept the unacceptable? Does it happen all at once? Little by little?   Accepting the unacceptable happens when you feel defeated. When you feel hopeless, that's when you surrender. No more! It's time to set healthy boundaries for your relationships and protect yourself.

To set personal boundaries, you have to decide what your needs are. What do you need to protect your individuality, needs, values, and goals? Boundaries can be emotional, physical, or even digital.

Personal Boundary Examples

- I'm cool with following each other on social media, but not with sharing passwords.
- I'm comfortable kissing and holding hands, but not in public.
- I'm okay with regularly texting, but I don't want to text multiple times in an hour.
- I want to spend time with my friends/family on weekends.
- I need quiet time to myself every day.
- I'm comfortable with some touching, but I'm not ready to have sex.

Decide what you need, then create boundaries around that. What do you need to feel emotionally and physically safe? It's helpful to think through your own boundaries, no matter what your relationship status is. Pay attention to how you feel about and react to situations, whether in real life or in things you watch on television.

What things make you uncomfortable? What's important to you? What do you want to keep private? Are there any behaviors or traits you will not tolerate (these are called dealbreakers)?

Create Your Boundaries

Write a list of boundaries. Don't worry about them being perfect. Just do your best.

_____

_____

_____

_____

_____

_____

_____

_____

_____

Increasing Your Expectations

Be confident and expect people to respond positively to your boundaries. When you're confident, you're practicing the first pillar of self-love. Self-confidence gives you the courage to believe that you deserve what you're asking of others. When you respect yourself by requiring others to respect you, your confidence increases, and you're also practicing the third pillar of self-love, which is self-respect.

Remember, your job isn't to convince people that you're worthy of being treated right; it's to love yourself enough to walk away when they don't. When people mistreat you remember this…they could've treated you right. They could've been the ones to heal your heart instead of breaking it. They could've loved you, just as you chose to love them. Don't waste any more time crying over them.

You don't lose anything when you let go of people who've hurt you. They do! Refuse to settle for rude, disrespectful, selfish, and insecure people. If you want healthy and happy relationships, you must first believe that you can have them. Never remove your boundaries to accommodate people who refuse to change. Boundaries are your protection; without them, you're defenseless. You don't owe people anything, but you owe yourself a lot. You owe yourself to do what's best for you, even if it angers those around you.

Actions Reveal How People Feel

How people treat you is how they feel about you. I used to listen to a person's words and get confused when their actions didn't line up. Now I know that it's not what someone says that matters; it's their actions. If they act like they don't like you, it's because they don't. If they don't make you a priority, it's because you're not. If they never keep their word, they don't want to. Stop overcomplicating relationships because you want to make them work. You're the only one trying.

Don't be willingly blind. That's asking for trouble. How many times does a person have to use you? How many times do they have to cheat on you and be disrespectful to you for you to understand that they don't deserve you! Stop waiting for people to do the absolute worst to you before you get the courage to remove them from your life.

When you tolerate disrespect, you're showing people that they can treat you like crap, and you'll still stay. People with good intentions won't allow themselves to get comfortable disrespecting you because they understand that love and disrespect can't abide together. If someone repeatedly disrespects you, it's a sign that they're not interested in loving you. They may want to use you, control you and manipulate you, but loving you is the furthest thing from their mind.

Disrespect is a sign that a person doesn't care about losing you; you're not valuable to them. You'll know this by their actions. You won't have to wonder if someone has changed. Their actions will speak for themselves. Don't settle for being an option when you could be a priority. You deserve to be prioritized. You deserve to feel valued. When a person values something, they treat it with care. They protect it. The same goes for relationships. People who love you will appreciate, respect, and protect you. I wish I had learned these lessons sooner than I did.

Have Your Own Back

As much as you want people to respect your boundaries, there is no guarantee that they ever will. Some of the people closest to you will disappoint you, hurt you, and disrespect you. You have to stop condoning their behavior. Go where you are valued and appreciated. As an adult, it's your responsibility to protect yourself from harmful people and things. Never depend on someone else to do it for you.

Take responsibility for your relationships and who you choose to have relationships with. Choose good people for you and your future, and let go of people who behave recklessly with your heart. Stop telling yourself that you can't let go of people because you love them. You don't know what love is if you've never learned how to love yourself.

Something needs to change if your life isn't better because someone is in it. Relationships should add to you, not drain you.

The only person you have the power to change is yourself. You can't change anyone no matter how much you love them or want them in your life. You're not asking for too much for expecting people to change their behavior when it negatively impacts you. They should do that because they care about you. The people who are meant to be in your life will correct any behavior that hurts you.

They will consider you before making choices that directly affect you. Don't believe anyone who tells you that changing is unreasonable or impossible. People change for the people they love and value.

Chapter 4 Review

Point 1:

Boundaries are necessary. They protect you. People who lack healthy boundaries are often violated and easily taken advantage of. Communicating your boundaries is essential when someone breaks them. People get to choose whether they respect your boundaries. When someone refuses to respect your boundaries, they're telling you that they are an unsafe person. If they are unwilling to change, you need to end the relationship. Creating healthy boundaries is essential for creating and maintaining healthy relationships; without them, you will suffer.

Point 2:

Setting boundaries is very personal. Your boundaries are based solely on what you need to feel respected and safe in your relationships. No one has the right to tell you what should or shouldn't be a boundary. Never let people be okay violating your boundaries. If they refuse to change, you need to end the relationship.

Point 3:

Confidence is necessary for setting and upholding your boundaries. If you don't feel worthy of what you're asking, you won't require others to give them to you. Base your boundaries on the treatment you need from the people you have relationships with.

Point 4:

How people treat you is how they feel about you. Don't spend your time confused. If a person's words don't match their actions, believe their actions. Decide what their actions reveal about the actual state of the relationships. You deserve someone sure about you. Don't settle for less.

Everyone is Replaceable

If you don't learn how to love yourself again, you'll hold on to relationships and lose yourself

There was a time when I thought I couldn't live without certain people. These same people mistreated me, told lies, and tried to sabotage my success. Through pain, hurt, and betrayal, I learned that I could live without anyone. Although I wish these things never happened, they taught me to depend on myself and trust God. People will disappoint you, but God is faithful. People will let you down, but you don't have to let yourself down.

Stop making people your source and let God be your source. I found peace knowing that I was completely loved and accepted by my heavenly father. He is the source of my joy, peace, and love. I suggest you let him be yours too. He's the only one who has never let me down.

The idea that you can't live without someone is why you stay in toxic situations. Don't give anyone that much power. You can live without anyone.

You have to be so in love with yourself that you refuse to be with anyone who doesn't make your life better. People who care about you want you to be happy. Toxic people are the ones who drain you and make your life miserable. Removing toxic people is essential to restore peace to your life.

When we let them go, we make room in our lives for the right people. Relationships are important because they affect every area of our lives, for better or for worse. If your relationships are safe and loving, you will feel safe and secure. Your life will be peaceful.

Pieces of Me
(Part 5)

Abandonment, Death, and
a Broken Foot

The ambulance came. The paramedic told me that my foot looked broken and that they could take me to the emergency room. I was alone with six kids, so I declined. Instead, They carried me downstairs and sat me on the couch. When they left, I called a family friend, and she came over. I tried calling my husband, but he didn't answer his phone.

Lights out at the homeless shelter was at nine o'clock, and it was way past nine. She drove to the shelter and picked him up. He stayed with the kids while she took me to the hospital. The doctor said it was a broken fibula. It was the first time I'd ever broken anything. My husband was forced to come home because he was the only one available to care for me. He was angry, and it showed.

That holiday season was the worst of my life. I needed help getting everywhere. The pain was so bad that I couldn't even walk. Every time I tried, it made my back hurt, so I decided to buy a wheelchair. The doctor said that my foot would take six to eight weeks to heal. The accident occurred the Sunday before Thanksgiving. I've always loved the holidays, so I was distraught.

Because of the accident, I assumed my husband would be making Thanksgiving dinner. I began talking to him about cooking, and he rudely said that I'd never asked him to make Thanksgiving dinner. I was perplexed.

He told me straight up that he wouldn't be cooking Thanksgiving dinner. I was upset, but what could I do? I felt helpless once again. That year I bought mostly boxed food. I cooked dinner rolling around in my office chair. I cooked with a broken foot and while nursing a six-month-old baby. I can't tell you how I held it together. Do you believe in God? It's the only way I can explain making it through that terrible time. After I spent the morning slaving over a hot stove he sat down and ate my Thanksgiving dinner guilt-free. I was repulsed.

You'd think cooking dinner with a broken foot was bad enough, but sadly, there's more. Christmas was just as bad. He threatened to leave every other day. He had a bad attitude and constant mood swings. I did all I could to keep a smile on my face and to not let the kids see me cry.

At home, I was constantly walking on eggshells. The very few times he was happy and playing with kids was when I was depressed and miserable from dealing with him. At those times, I would glance over at him, and I could swear I could see a slight grin on his face.

At a Christmas party we attended with the kids, he was pushing me through the door in my wheelchair and it got caught on the bump at the bottom. The wheelchair hit the bump so hard that I almost flew off with my youngest son in my hands. The second time he rammed my wheelchair even harder. The guy in the doorway saw it and spoke up. I was so embarrassed I wanted to disappear. I felt stuck!

I hoped no one I knew recognized me. Afterward, he didn't apologize or change his behavior. He walked around like he owned the world. I wanted to leave, but I didn't have the courage. Months later, we were still in marriage counseling. It didn't help. It just gave him another person to lie to and manipulate. It certainly didn't change his behavior.

One day, he switched lanes swiftly without signaling on the way home from a session, which scared me. I asked him not to do that because of my experience of my ex kidnaping me in a car (I describe it in detail in Love Yourself First). When I told him this, he said that I wasn't going to tell him what to do. He then pulled the car over, got out, and said that he was going to the courthouse to file for divorce. I begged him to stay, but he refused.

I was shocked, confused, and emotionally distraught. Two of our small children were in the car at the time. I called a friend, and she tried to comfort me. She told me that he would destroy my life if I didn't leave him. It was the first time anyone spoke so straightforwardly about the reality of my situation. I knew she was right. I had to leave, but when, where, how? ...*To be continued.*

Recognizing Toxicity

Toxic people show us they're toxic long before our hearts get involved. We often ignore the signs and proceed to our hurt instead of protecting ourselves as we should. Toxic people know they're unhealthy, but they don't want to change. They want you and I to accept them as they are. Their past relationships failed because of the same problems, but they still refused to address them. Instead of changing, they blame others to avoid taking responsibility.

Don't be the person who has to learn things the hard way. When toxic people show you who they are, believe them. Don't try to talk them into changing for you you. If they won't be better for themselves, they don't deserve you! Know what you want, and don't settle for less.

If you don't like smoking, don't date smokers. Don't date someone irresponsible with money if you want a financially responsible spouse. If you want a man who will be a good father, then don't date someone who doesn't take care of the children they already have. Things are a lot simpler than we make them.

If someone is short-tempered or controlling at the beginning of a relationship, that's who they are. Don't make excuses for them.

Don't think their behavior is accidental. It's intentional. Don't risk your life by being with someone unsafe or unstable. Protect yourself and exit the relationship quickly. The sooner you leave, the easier it will be. The longer you stay, the more complicated and dangerous it will become.

Make no friendship with an angry man, and with a furious man, thou shalt not go.
-Proverbs 22:24

People Unwilling to Pay the Price

If someone wants something bad enough, they'll pay whatever it costs. Respect and consistency is the price someone must pay to be in your life. It's not a punishment; it's an honor. If someone is unwilling to meet your requirements, they don't deserve to have you. Never put yourself on the clearance rack, hoping someone will choose you. You are worthy of everything you're asking for. Value doesn't go on sale.

Stop going all out for people who don't reciprocate. If you're the only one putting in the effort in your relationship, stop! You might want that person, but that person doesn't want you. I know it's hard to hear, but the reason we waste so much time in relationships is that we want to believe that people are someone they're not.

People are always telling us who they are, but the problem is that we seldom believe them.

It's unwise to give toxic people access to you. You must value yourself more. Why do you think celebrities and high-profile people are hard to get close to? Most times, you have to know someone in their inner circle to get in contact with them. It's because they see their time and presence as valuable.

Likewise, you must see yourself as valuable too. The people in your inner circle should have your back. Those aren't your people if you have to wonder if they talk about you when you leave the room. You have to be honest with yourself, even if it means having to let people go. I know you want them to be in your life, but that's a choice they have to make by treating you right.

People have to want to be the best versions of themselves. If not, they'll make you miserable. The deciding factor shouldn't be if you love someone; it should be...do they love you? Do they make your life better or worse? Do they add to your life or subtract from it? These essential questions will help you decide if you're holding on to people you should let go of.

Holding onto toxic people is like carrying fire; eventually, you will get burned.

Can a man carry fire next to his chest and his clothes not be burned? Or can one walk on hot coals and his feet not be scorched?
-Proverbs 6:27-28 (ESV)

Giving & Getting Nothing

Why do we give so much to people who give us so little in return? They take and take, and we keep on giving. These relationships are typical with people who have little concern for our mental and emotional health. Where did we learn that other people's needs were more important than our own? Unlearn that! Don't keep the peace by destroying your own. You deserve relationships with people who care about your well-being.

Just because people have let you down doesn't mean you have to keep letting yourself down. Anyone unwilling to invest good energy into the relationship doesn't deserve a place in your life. You're not a doormat! Relationships were never meant to be life-sucking experiences. We have the freedom to choose who we have in our life. These people should make us feel safe and challenge us to be better. They shouldn't make us feel insecure or confused.

Stop giving your best to people who give you the worst of them.

When people claiming to love you mistreat you, it's a clear sign that they don't respect you. I'm sorry if no one ever told you this. Don't let it devastate you. Let it teach you. Let it prepare you for next time. Often we take things so personally, believing that someone's refusal to love us or treat us right means that we aren't worthy of their love. The opposite is true: they aren't worthy of your love!

People tell us how they feel about us with their actions. It's time we start listening. If you stop and take your time, you will see everything you need to know and where you stand with people. Don't waste years trying to figure out if someone wants to be in your life. Stop giving people all the options and leaving yourself with none. You may want them, but you don't need them.

Don't be desperate for anyone's company; learn to love your own. Go where you are wanted and appreciated. How will you know? It will be unmistakable. You will feel it, see it and experience it.

Don't Love Unconditionally

When people use you, abuse you and mistreat you, you have a right to be angry and walk away. Let it make you smarter and wiser. How? By learning from your mistakes and turning that angry energy into self-love energy. If they choose not to love you, the least you can do is love yourself.

Use that energy for your good. Please don't waste it on them. You have power! The power to accept people as they are, the power to love people and still let them go. Choose what's best for you even when it hurts.

Never hold on to people who've decided that you're not worthy of being treated right. You'll know it. Please don't ignore it. People choose who they want to be. Just because they're okay disrespecting you doesn't mean you have to be. You will always be discontent in toxic relationships because you know you deserve better.

You don't owe people opportunities to hurt you. Stop giving people chance after chance to break your heart. People who don't appreciate you made their choice. They decided to take you for granted, and you shouldn't take that lightly. Remember, how they treat you is how they feel about you. It's not a mistake. It's intentional.

You weren't put on this earth to suffer. Just because you were treated poorly in the past doesn't mean you have to continue to accept poor treatment now. You have the freedom to choose. People who want you to accept bad behavior are the ones you need to run from. People who love you don't take pleasure in seeing you suffer. They want you to be whole and happy. Choosing to stay with someone who is hurting you is dangerous. Don't let fear of losing people cause you to hold onto relationships that are harming you.

You can love someone, miss them, and still move on simultaneously.

You don't have to bow or bend to meet the needs of self-centered, unreasonable, and irrational people. Stop sacrificing yourself for people who won't sacrifice anything for you. Let them go so that you can make room for the right people in your life. Relationships should be safe places for you to grow. Your closest relationships should be the most loving and supportive.

Never continue relationships with people who are always critical. If you're not good enough for them, you'll be good enough for someone else. Don't waste your time. I know this is hard, but hard doesn't mean impossible. It also doesn't mean settle. This is why most people waste time in crappy, unfulfilling relationships. Don't let this be you. Don't change who you are to please other people. There's nothing wrong with you; They're not right for you. It's time to let them go!

Chapter 5 Review

Point 1:

You can live without anybody. People who mistreat you aren't worthy of your time and attention. Although it may hurt to leave someone you care about, you have to decide to do what's best for you. Staying in a toxic relationship has no benefits. You deserve real love. You deserve to be safe and happy. The people you love should love you just as much as you love them. Don't settle for less.

Point 2:

You can't depend on other people to be your source. You have to let you and God be your source. The only person you can't live without is you. Don't let people drive you to the end of yourself trying to love them. Stop chasing after love and become the love you want to experience. Whatever love looks like to you, do that. You are worthy of love.

Point 3:

Recognize toxic people and don't make excuses for them. Toxic people know that their behavior is unhealthy; they want you to accept them as they are. When you see someone is only concerned about themselves, you have to follow their lead and only be worried about yourself. Stop waiting for people's hearts to change towards you. Stop begging for love. You're not an animal. Leave them and never let them come back. They don't deserve another chance.

Point 4:

Stop giving your love to people who refuse to reciprocate. You deserve better than that! If someone doesn't appreciate what you bring to the table, then leave the table. You don't have to convince anyone that you deserve their love. If they don't recognize value, you don't need them in your life. Love yourself and move on. Don't love people unconditionally. Love people who love you in return.

6

Loved, Despite Who Didn't Love You

If you don't learn how to love yourself again, you'll spend the rest of your life crying over who left you

It's not about who left you or who didn't love you. It's about loving, valuing, and honoring yourself despite it and cherishing yourself the way you want to be cherished. Loving yourself the way you want to be loved and refusing to settle for less than you deserve. Stop wasting your time worrying about who left you, hurt you, lied to you, and broke your heart. They've moved on with their life, and it's time you moved on with yours.

You are loved, worthy, and valuable. You wouldn't have settled if you knew then what you know now. Learn from your mistakes, and don't beat yourself up over them. I know it's unfair. I know you think they got away with it, but they didn't. People reap what they sow. Don't spend your time worrying about the people in your past. Focus on your present.

Focus on where you're going, not where you've been. Focus on how far you've come, not on how far you have to go. Please don't believe the lie that it's too late for you. Don't stay stuck out of fear. You can have the love you've always wanted. It begins with believing you can.

I heard someone say: we love hard because it was hard not being loved. When we've experienced pain, we create ways to avoid being hurt again. If we're not careful, this turns into people-pleasing to avoid conflict. We stay and love harder instead of leaving relationships when red flags appear.

Instead of setting boundaries, we make exceptions, hoping that the person we love will love us in return.

Pieces of Me
(Part 6)

Assault, Pregnancy & The Last Supper

The holiday season ended, and I was grateful it was over. I hoped the new year brought something better, but it was more of the same. Summertime rolled around, and the drama increased. Maybe God was trying to tell me something.

I spent my birthday celebrating myself as usual. A month later, my mom and I spent her birthday stealing my car back from my husband. I had asked him to leave because I needed a chance to breathe. Every time he left, I felt immediate peace. As soon as he returned, so did the drama. I took the house keys and locked the door behind me.

He was mentally and emotionally draining me, and it was all I could do to protect myself. He left and decided to take the car with him. For three days, I called him, trying to get the car back. He never answered. I had no way of going to the grocery store to buy food. What would I do if there was an emergency?

I called my mom and told her what was happening. She came over, and we spent the day driving around looking for my car. We found it a few hours later. Later that day, the police came to the house because he reported it stolen. I explained the ordeal to the policewoman, and she said he needed to grow up and stop acting stupid. She said that no charges would be filed and that she would let him know that I had it. That was the end of June. He came back to the house shortly after.

The Fourth of July came and went, and the neighbors were still lighting fireworks. One evening he decided to take the kids outside to watch. When he came back inside, his mood had changed. I sat on the couch with our two youngest sleeping on my lap. He came in, slammed the door, and began yelling. He was trying to start an argument with me.

I asked him to calm down and be quiet because the kids were sleeping, but he ignored me and proceeded to yell. There was a small table lamp behind my head, and he asked me to turn it off. I told him no because I was using it. When I refused, he snatched it up, held it over my head, and threatened me with it. He demanded I put the kids down. I told him no, but he kept insisting.

I can't explain the peace that came over me at that moment. It was supernatural. I calmly grabbed my phone and called the police. After I reported him, he threw his house keys at my face and went outside to wait for the police. My reflexes quickly kicked in and caught them before they hit me.

The police came, and he lied about threatening me with the lamp and throwing the keys at my face. He told them he was trying to turn the light off. They said that they couldn't press charges because no assault happened. Instead, they offered to take him to some other place. He left, and I didn't plan on letting him come back.

I later found out that he asked to be taken to a mental institution for an evaluation. He said they diagnosed him with bipolar depression. He never supplied me or anyone else with any evidence of his diagnosis, even though I asked him several times. He was a master manipulator and a liar. He was a professional victim, and he knew how to play his cards. I didn't care at this point. I was done. It had to end.

There was nothing good about this marriage. There was no benefit in staying. I knew if I stayed that it would eventually destroy me. I deserved better than that. I now knew that he would never give it to me. I'm not too fond of the saying; all good things must end because it's not good that needs to end; it's the bad, the ugly, and the toxic.

This marriage was over before it began. I just wasn't able to see it. The signs were always there, warning me. I just saw them as something else. He crossed every line. This relationship had taken me lower than I ever thought I could go. I could no longer fake it.

I would've never believed it if I hadn't gone through it. I filed for divorce later that week. That summer was the hardest of my life. Learning to be a single mom of six was challenging to say the least. I counted the days until school started. Some mornings all I could do was lie in bed until I had no choice but to get up. It wasn't easy, but I did it. I was proud of myself.

The week he left, I enrolled in a domestic violence support group. I knew that I needed all the support I could get. September came, and I got used to the routine, but I was exhausted. When I'd call my husband to ask for help with the kids, he said he was working. My lowest point was sitting in my car and crying because he said he was coming to help but never came. I wondered if my children were better off being raised by someone else. I felt hopeless.

The holidays got closer, and he started showing up again. He began offering to help with the kids. Would he finally be the man I needed him to be? I fell for it hook line and sinker. Six weeks later, I discovered that I was pregnant. He was still out of the house, and I fell into a depression. I started going to therapy to get help. I felt so stupid for falling for his tricks again. I spent a lot of time blaming and shaming myself. I knew I had to get out of the mental and emotional rut I was in.

That's when I decided to turn the pain I had experienced into something positive, something that could help someone else. I decided to do what I did best: create. I began writing Love Yourself First. I threw myself into writing that book. I wrote when the kids were at school, while the little ones napped, and after I put the kids to bed. Some nights I stayed up until three o'clock in the morning writing. I thought of all the lessons I had learned and what I wished I would've known years ago.

Writing that book and my relationship with God saved my life. Then COVID-19 happened, the schools were shut down, and I was pregnant and tired. I decided to let him come back temporarily to help during my pregnancy. I told him that he could stay, but he would have to leave after the baby was born. I watched and looked for signs of change during that time, but he was still the same man. I was unmoved.

The baby came via emergency c-section. Maybe all the stress had finally caught up with me. All six of my other children were natural unmedicated births. The recovery was long and painful. He was even worse. I had to take care of myself on many occasions when he'd act like it was too much to make me breakfast or do a simple task.

What was the point of having him around? It seemed like the only thing he knew how to do was get me pregnant. I felt like Abigail in the Bible, married to a foolish and wicked man. Thanksgiving rolled around, and he was still there. He didn't lift a finger to help cook even though I had a newborn and was recovering from major surgery.

As I watched him devour my Thanksgiving dinner, I plotted how to get him out of my house. I promised myself that he would never eat my Thanksgiving dinner again. It was his last supper.

A few days later, as I was praying for strength, I asked God for an exit plan. He told me: I Am the Plan. That afternoon I told him to leave. I wasn't angry or upset. I was finished. I had no ill feelings, but I was determined not to celebrate another Christmas or New Year with him. He had ruined enough special occasions.

There was no arguing, no fighting, just peace. By the look on his face, I could tell that he knew I was serious when I told him. His reign of terror was over. I needed to heal, and that could never happen as long as he was around. Sometimes the best decisions are the hardest ones to make. Make them anyway.

You may have to ugly cry. Ugly cry and do what you need to do. You deserve healing. You deserve wholeness. Please give it to yourself.

Self-Love Isn't Easy, but it's Possible

Whoever said that self-love is easy was lying. Self-love isn't shopping sprees, facials, pedicures, and massages. That can be a part of it, but real self-love is doing what's best for you even when it's difficult; that's true love. Self-love is challenging, uncomfortable, messy, and inconvenient. It's hard because it requires you to make tough decisions. It involves work that will challenge your thoughts, behaviors, and beliefs.

It requires you to love yourself even when you don't feel lovable. It requires you to let go of things you want to hold on to. Sometimes it doesn't feel easy to love yourself because the people that should've loved you didn't. Love yourself anyway. Although self-love is hard, the alternative is worse.

Tolerating disrespect and mistreatment will eventually take their toll on you. It's not worth it. No one is worth your health and peace. You deserve better even if you've never experienced it. You deserve better even if you feel unworthy. You deserve better even if others don't think you do.

You've been committed to others. It's time to commit to yourself. You've loved others, don't tell me you can't love yourself. It may be challenging, but it's possible.

The version of you that's confident, secure, and loving yourself will take time to create. When you love someone, you don't just do what's easy; you do what's necessary. When you love someone, you do what's best for them. You put boundaries in place to keep them safe. You protect their mental, emotional and physical health. You make sacrifices for them. That someone is you. Invest in yourself.

Loving yourself again means learning who you are and what you need to live a joyful, peaceful, satisfying life. Why should everyone benefit from you except you? Don't miss out. There's a life waiting for you better than you ever imagined. It starts with falling in love with yourself and learning how to become everything you want and need.

From this place of self-fullness, you'll begin to develop the confidence to create the life and relationships you desire. Become the thing you want, and the thing you want will find you.

20 Practical Ways to Love Yourself Again

1. Go to therapy

2. Remove toxic people from your life

3. Schedule a massage

4. Get a pedicure

5. Invest in your retirement account

6. Eat healthier

7. Go out to eat with supportive and positive friends

8. Turn off your phone without worrying

9. Take a nap

10. Go for a walk

11. Ignore negative calls & texts

12. Block toxic people on social media

13. Say no without apologizing

14. Take a bath

15. Go to sleep early

16. Watch your favorite movie

17. Hire a babysitter

18. Do nothing without feeling guilty

19. Tell someone no (just because you don't want to)

20. Apologize to yourself for the way people treated you and for the bad things that have happened to you

Self-love is personal. What are 5 ways you can show love to yourself this week? Write them down below:

1._____

2._____

3._____

4._____

5._____

The Importance of Confidence

People who mistreat others are often extremely insecure. They use their poor treatment of others to mask their pain-confidence isn't arrogant. Self-confidence is having faith in yourself and your abilities. It means treating yourself well and requiring others to do the same. If you're tired of not being loved, you need to focus on loving yourself.

You let others believe that they didn't have to do much to get you or keep you in the past. You allowed others to get comfortable disappointing you. You accepted poor treatment, and they were happy to give it to you. No more! The wrong ones will leave you, but the right ones will always stay.

Have faith that good people are waiting to love you. They're looking forward to treating you right. How you think is important. If you believe you're damaged goods, you'll let others treat you like it. The way you think about yourself will affect the way you feel. The way you feel will affect the things you do. The things you do will attract or repel people.

When you love yourself, you won't allow others to mistreat you. If someone mistreats you, you'll see it as their loss. You won't blame yourself or have any reservations about removing them from your life. It might be challenging, but you'll do it anyway. Don't let people with confidence issues make you feel insecure about believing yourself.

Don't let insecure people make you feel guilty for believing in yourself. Don't let anyone rob you of your confidence. You're going to need confidence for everything you accomplish in life. Ignore the haters and keep doing you. Self-confidence changes how you think: You're not looking for someone; someone is looking for you. You're not waiting for love; someone is waiting to love you.

This newfound mindset will change your energy, countenance, and experience.

Shut Up & Love Yourself

There will always be something that makes you feel unworthy of self-love. The voices telling you you're not good enough don't matter anymore. I want you to shut up and love yourself despite how you feel! Shut up the excuses. Shut up the lies. Shut up the opinions. Shut up the fears! Just shut up, and love yourself (insert smile).

Hug yourself. Compliment yourself. Do something nice for yourself. You don't need permission to love and respect yourself. Let the light of self-love in! You've been walking in the dark too long. You've been waiting for love long enough. It's your turn to be whole. Receive the healing that comes from believing in your worthiness. Don't be concerned about offending people. God is with you, and you will not fail.

At times loving yourself may feel uncomfortable. You'll wonder if you should settle like those around you. Please don't do it. Love yourself harder, push further and keep going. Believe in yourself, and don't quit.

I see you rising from the ashes. I see you smiling. I see you laughing. I see you living your best life. I see you happier than ever before, all because you decided to...Love Yourself Again!

Chapter 6 Review

Point #1:

It doesn't matter who left you or who didn't love you. You are loved despite this. Loving yourself again is all about loving yourself the way you want to be loved, cherishing yourself the way you want to be cherished, and not letting your bad experiences define you. You are worthy of love. You are worthy of affection. Don't wait for another second to be loved by someone else. Love yourself instead.

Point #2:

Self-love requires work. It challenges us to make better decisions instead of the ones we're familiar with. It requires us to stand up for ourselves and confront people and circumstances that undermine our worth and value. It calls us to prioritize our mental and emotional health over other people's feelings and opinions. Self-love is hard, but it's always worth it.

Point #3:

Confidence is necessary on your journey to loving yourself. You need confidence to believe in yourself and to give yourself what you need. It takes confidence to set standards, create boundaries, and walk in self-love. Some days will be easier than others, but don't throw in the towel. Keep doing you.

Point #4:

There will be an excuse not to love yourself. Your insecurities, imperfections, and past mistakes are a few reasons you may feel unworthy. Love yourself anyway. Stop waiting for perfection to love all of yourself. Love yourself where you're at and work on where you want to be. Don't settle out of comfort. Put in the work to be who you want to be and to create the life you want to live.

The Self-Love Pledge

I _____ pledge to love, respect and honor myself. I pledge to be for me and not against me. I pledge only to be loyal to those who are loyal to me. I will honor myself by listening to my intuition. I pledge to be my greatest supporter and my biggest fan. I will forgive myself when I make mistakes. I will do what's best for me, even when it's hard.

I pledge to love myself utilizing The Four Pillars of Self-Love: Self-Confidence, Self-Development, Self-Respect & Self-Preservation. I will not live in the past. I will not hold onto people out of fear. I pledge never to abandon myself to chase after others. I will never give up on myself. I am worthy of everything I want, including real love.

Sign:_____

Ready for Love

Ready for love

But all I got was pain

Ready for love

But I gave it in vain

Ready for love

But all I got was shame

Ready for love

But all I got was blame

Ready for love

Now I can finally see

Ready for love

I was really waiting on me

Ready for love

Now that I've learned to be my own best friend

Ready for love

I'm gonna love myself again

About the Author

Krystle Laughter is an author, mentor, speaker, and certified life coach. She is the mother of seven and creator of Krystle Laughter Academy, an online school for women to heal, learn and grow. Her goal is to empower and educate women about the life-changing power of self-love. Krystle has triumphed to become the woman she is today, overcoming homelessness and domestic violence. She has written many books, including The Love Yourself Series and He Doesn't Love You If. She is also an author consultant who helps other people write and publish their books. Follow her on social media to learn more.

Krystle Laughter Academy

The 24-Hour Author Coming 2022

Self-Love 101 Online Course

After Toxic Online Course

BOOKS

The Love Yourself Series
Get All 4 Books Today!

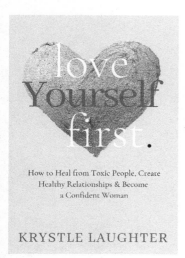

Love Yourself First

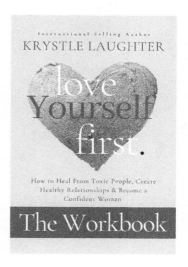

The Workbook

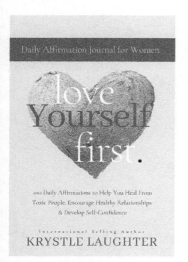

The Affirmation Journal

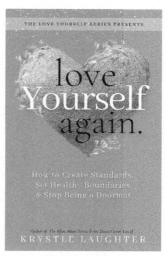

Love Yourself Again

Now Available!

He Doesn't Love You If...
10 Signs He's Not Serious About You
& is Wasting Your Time

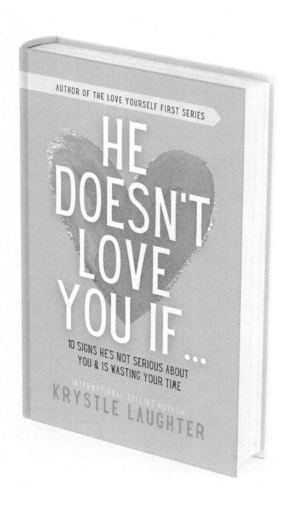

Now Available!

You're a Diamond:
A 30-Day Devotional for Women

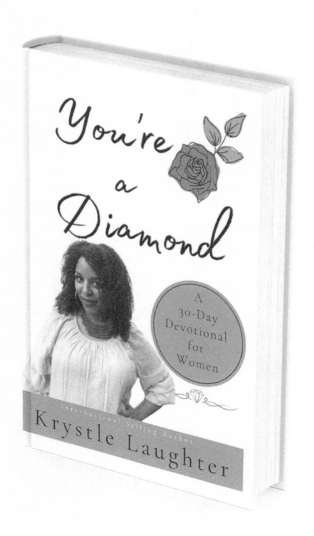

Now Available!

Self-Love Everyday:
31 Empowering Affirmations

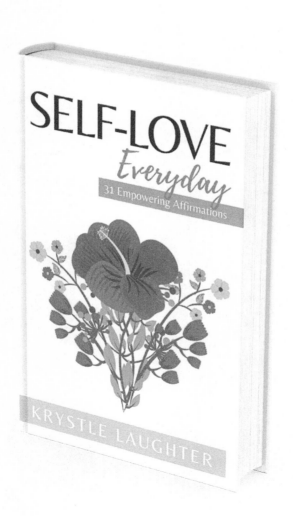

The AFTER ABUSE SERIES

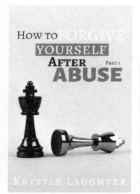

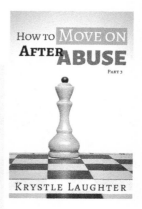

Coming 2022

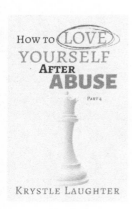

Children's Books

Get Them All Today on Amazon!!

MUSIC

All Things New

Krystle provides soulful, uplifting, and inspirational melodies to elevate your spirit. From Somebody Say O' to He Can't Love You Like Jesus. This music will speak to your heart, mind & soul. Get her music on CdBaby or Amazon today!

Made in the USA
Coppell, TX
20 January 2022

71996267R00090